W9-BSH-591

WORLD OF INSECTS

Cicadas

by Colleen Sexton

BELLWETHER MEDIA • MINNEAPOLIS, MN

Note to Librarians, Teachers, and Parents:

Blastoff! Readers are carefully developed by literacy experts and combine standards-based content with developmentally appropriate text.

Level 1 provides the most support through repetition of high-frequency words, light text, predictable sentence patterns, and strong visual support.

Level 2 offers early readers a bit more challenge through varied simple sentences, increased text load, and less repetition of high-frequency words.

Level 3 advances early-fluent readers toward fluency through increased text and concept load, less reliance on visuals, longer sentences, and more literary language.

Whichever book is right for your reader, Blastoff! Readers are the perfect books to build confidence and encourage a love of reading that will last a lifetime!

This edition first published in 2007 by Bellwether Media.

No part of this publication may be reproduced in whole or in part without written permission of the publisher. For information regarding permission, write to Bellwether Media Inc., Attention: Permissions Department, Post Office Box 1C, Minnetonka, MN 55345-9998.

Library of Congress Cataloging-in-Publication Data
Sexton, Colleen A.
   Cicadas / by Colleen Sexton.
      p. cm. — (World of insects)
Summary: "Simple text accompanied by full-color photographs give an upclose look at cicadas. Intended for kindergarten through third grade students"—Provided by publisher.
   Includes bibliographical references and index.
   ISBN-13: 978-1-60014-051-8 (hardcover : alk. paper)
   ISBN-10: 1-60014-051-3 (hardcover : alk. paper)
   1. Cicadas—Juvenile literature. I. Title.

   QL527.C5S49 2007
   595.7'52—dc22   2006034961

Contents

It is a warm summer day. A loud buzzing comes from the trees.

That sound is male cicadas **singing**.

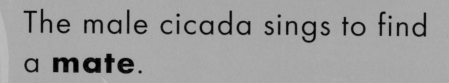

The male cicada sings to find a **mate**.

Males sing in summer when females are ready to lay eggs.

The female chooses a twig
and cuts a small slit in it.

eggs

She lays her eggs in the slit.

Nymphs hatch from the eggs. They are small and do not have wings.

The nymphs fall from the tree to the ground. They dig holes into the soil.

The nymphs grow slowly
under the ground. They
shed their **skin** many times.

The nymphs dig to the top of the soil when they are grown.

The nymphs shed their skin one more time. They leave their skin on a tree trunk.

Adult cicadas are big **insects**.

All insects have six legs.

small eyes

big eyes

Cicadas have two big eyes and three small eyes. They can see well.

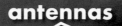

antennas

Cicadas have **antennas**.
They use their antennas to
feel and smell things.

mouth

Cicadas have a mouth shaped like a straw. They suck plant **sap** through this tube.

Cicadas have four wings.

They unfold their wings to fly away.

Glossary

antennas—the feelers on an insect's head; insects use their antennas to touch and smell things.

insect—a small animal with six legs and a hard outer body that is divided into three parts; most insects also have two or four wings.

mate—a male or female member of a pair of animals; male cicadas sing to find a female mate.

nymph—a young insect without wings. Cicada nymphs stay under the ground for many years before they are grown. Cicada nymphs must grow and shed their skin many times before they finally become adults.

sap—a watery juice that runs inside of plants; sap carries food for the plant.

singing—making musical sounds; male cicadas use special organs called tymbals to sing.

skin—the outside covering of the body; cicadas have a tough outer shell called an exoskeleton.

To Learn More

AT THE LIBRARY

Hall, Margaret. *Cicadas*. Mankato, Minn.: Pebble Books, 2006.

Macken, JoAnn Early. *The Life Cycle of a Cicada*. Milwaukee, Wisc.: Gareth Stevens, 2006.

Ryder, Joanne. *When the Woods Hum*. New York: Morrow Junior Books, 1991.

Squire, Ann O. *Cicadas*. New York: Children's Press, 2003.

ON THE WEB

Learning more about cicadas is as easy as 1, 2, 3.

1. Go to www.factsurfer.com

2. Enter "cicadas" into search box.

3. Click the "Surf" button and you will see a list of related web sites.

With factsurfer.com, finding more information is just a click away.

Index

The photographs in this book are reproduced through the courtesy of: Priscilla R. Steele, front cover, p. 5; Olga Lyubkina, p. 4; Daniel Dempster Photography/Alamy, pp. 6; Rodney Mehring, p. 7; Nature's Planet Museum/ACollection/Getty Images, p. 8; Bryan Carpenter, pp. 9, 9(inset), 11; Graphic Science/Alamy, p. 10; Rena Schild, pp. 12, 20; Darlyne A Murawski/Getty Images, pp. 13, 19, 21; Cheong Seng Fui, p. 14; Tim Quade, p. 15; Vladimir Ivanov, p. 16; Sandra Caldwell, p. 17; Jonathan Larsen, p. 18.